False Prophecies, Reassessing Buddha and the Call to the Second Cognition

By

Endall Beall

Second Edition

Copyright © 2016 Endall Beall
All Rights Reserved
ISBN 13: 978-1535091039
ISBN 10: 1535091037

Dedication

This book is dedicated to all the true spirit warriors who have not given up on themselves despite all the disappointments.

Table of Contents

       Acknowledgments
xiii. - Foreword
1.   - Introduction
3.   - 1. The Great Disappointment
12. - 2. The Real Story of Siddhartha Guatama
21. - 3. Recovering from Cognitive Dissonance
29. - 4. The Mission
35. - 5. Turning the System Around

ACKNOWLEDGEMENTS

I want to thank Rob Mirage for graciously providing the photo that adorns the cover of this book. I also wish to acknowledge Kacy Ryan who provided her perspectives by writing the Foreword to this Second Edition release. You both have my heartfelt gratitude for your contributions to this volume.

I would also like to thank my spiritual companions who have stood by me as they worked to advanced into their own cognitive awareness. It has not been an easy road for any of us.

FOREWORD

When I first came across Endall Beall's extremely radical series of books, the contents of which threatened to turn my lifelong pursuit of spiritual truth into a folly, I felt a strong need to know how they came into being. What could have possibly informed them and why on earth should I trust them? I was actually quite outraged by the irreverent audacity of the first book I bought, so outraged, in fact, that I gave it a negative one star review on Amazon (which I've subsequently deleted).

Where had the information come from that stated, most unequivocally, that the entire body of 'spiritual' teachings humans had bought into was a fabrication, its presence on our planet no more than the viciously deceptive tactic of malevolent off world beings? Unabashed, the books inverted the entire spiritual canon of our world, an inversion of something so intrinsic, so all encompassing and so archaic, it seemed outrageous.

That said, I gave up on religion in my childhood and moved to reading the books of Doris Stokes who 'spoke to the dead' and Rosemary Brown who wrote not very good music supposedly transmitted by famous deceased composers. As a student in London, the crossed legs, dawn risings and daunting disciplines of Buddhism became another alternative, eventually transpiring to be as futile as religion had proved to be and definitely not worth the pain, tiredness or effort involved. The age old Buddhist teachings obviously didn't work for me, though I assumed it was my fault rather than Buddha's. In my mid-twenties, enthralled by the annual 'Mind Body Spirit' exhibitions, I latched onto the New Age beliefs, plowing through 'spiritual' books *ad infinitum*, including Blavatsky's *Isis Unveiled* and *The Secret Doctrine* plus every single book Alice Bailey produced.

Through the written word, the New Age movement brought an ever increasing smorgasbord of tantalizing messages promising imminent global transformation. Themes of love; light; predicted events and changes; beneficent White Brotherhoods; the universal 'Oneness of God'; Angelic connections etc. abounded and Masters of Wisdom poured forth their knowledge through a proliferation of channeled messages which, though contradictory, ran easily down the paths of least resistance in the avid followers, who trusted them implicitly.

For all their prognosticating, however, over time it became apparent that the Masters didn't seem able to 'put their money where their mouth was' when it came to anything more than words. Nothing was transpiring beyond, of course, a bit of synchronicity here and there, which kept some people happy. Cataclysmic predictions or beatific promises came to nothing and transformation remained glued to the page. The non-event of 21st December 2012 was probably, for most, the final disappointment which drew the line in the sands of credibility for New Age prophecies.

That the world around us was overtly getting worse by the minute was simply being explained away as the death throes of the old before the dawn of the new, i.e. "It has to get worse before it gets better". Other explanations gullibly swallowed by stalwart New Agers were either that there was a mix up with spiritual time and earthly time or that mankind wasn't responding as quickly as had been hoped...which should have come as no surprise.

After the waning of religion, possibly due to the atrocities of two world wars damaging the cultural belief in an all loving God, the New Age had arrived on the scene like the New Black. Although I'd become deeply cynical and thoroughly disillusioned with the whole 'spiritual' thing, I decided to splash out on just one of Endall Beall's books, soon finding myself scathing of its sledgehammer approach. Not throwing the baby out with the bath water, I ordered another which impressed me so much I carried on buying them until I had practically the whole series. They were seriously unsettling, yet a part of me thought 'why not?'.

There was no mincing of words in Beall's acutely direct vernacular which, after an initial adjustment, I found extremely refreshing following decades of reading what had increasingly proved to be a *cul de sac* of impotent, platitudinous nonsense. In Endall Beall's straight to the point writing I began to sense a seed that was potently fertile. By now, I reckoned I could handle the content of the books shattering the beliefs that were underpinning my life but still I needed to be assured that the person responsible for bringing about such a 'destruction' was, in reality, to be trusted. At that point, I decided to make contact with Endall Beall, beginning a dialogue which soon made it blatantly evident to me that the author of this controversial and iconoclastic output was, in my grandma's words, 'straight as a die'. I found him to be a solidly sane man with no pretence at all, whose unwavering intention was to alert people to the tyranny and deception which has been the totality of humanity's story.

His commitment was evident in the hours of time he spent talking to me and in every word he spoke. I'm writing this foreword because I am aware that those who, like me, couldn't just settle within the reductionism and materialism of their times, and who found themselves on a long quest for 'the deeper truth', will probably have reflected my own path in many ways, as they were similarly dependent on the information or 'revelations' available.

So, what of this book in the context of all of this? Endall Beall has arrived on the scene not to stop the spiritual paradigm boat from sinking but to blow it, once and for all, out of the water, not on the back of misguided hubris or spiritual hedonism but simply as a practical and necessary action. This book was written to offer information that supports the authentic realization of the self and to replace the appealing but delusional 'spiritual' claptrap which has saturated and claimed the minds of the majority of decent and honest seekers of truth with something which has a real chance of bringing the much needed change we are all looking for. The book is very easy to read. I can only suggest you try it, and take it from there.

Kacy Ryan, UK, 2016

INTRODUCTION

The world stood in expectation of great things happening on December 21, 2012 predicated on all the hype surrounding the predictions of the Mayan Calendar. There was no shortage of books written by doomsayers decrying the end of the world as we know it, as well as a large supply of writers hyping some mystical shift in human consciousness that would magically make all the troubles of the world disappear and turn humanity into something different.

People in the arena of spiritual pursuits sat with baited breath for midnight on the projected date anxiously waiting for some kind of cosmic magic wand to be waved that would take us all into some kind of perceived spiritual utopia, harkening the dawn of a new age of mankind through some mystical form of a collective shift in human consciousness. The day came and went without notice, and the staunch believers in the Mayan prophecy were left holding a huge bag of disappointment. The world of December 22, 2012 was no different than the world the day before, except the grand excitement over this anticipated spiritual awakening didn't happen. This seminal event, or shall we call it a non-event, left most spiritual seekers in the lurch with no place to turn to focus their efforts on spiritual advancement.

Many people just threw in the towel and moved on, but genuine seekers trying to understand spirit were left with little to no explanation from their touted gurus about why all their mystical hype failed to manifest. Many of these gurus slunk away in shame and have not reared their heads since the great 2012 Disappointment. In light of this non-event, many spiritual seekers experienced a form of cognitive dissonance and have been left at sea where their mystical spiritual pursuits are concerned. This book is designed to show the genuine seeker that the spirit path is still wide open and that we do not need mystical prophecies and supernatural hype to succeed in our spiritual advancement either individually or as a species.

1. The Great Disappointment

For the sake of providing examples of disappointing non-events, we only have to look at the purported return of Jesus to find a windfall of failed calculations. If you check Wikipedia under 'predictions and claims for the Second Coming of Christ' and you will find more than 40 failed predictions since Christianity was invented. Probably the best known is what is called The Great Disappointment surrounding the Millerite movement in 1844 where the Baptist preacher William Miller proclaimed that Jesus would return to the Earth in 1844.

When Miller first proposed this return of Jesus theory he didn't find many takers, but eventually his projections about the imminent return of Jesus turned into a national phenomenon, not much unlike the 2012 Mayan prophecies. Exactly as with the 2012 hype, the closer the date came, the more printed matter was circulated to increase the hype about the proposed event. The Millerites evangelized their imminent return of Jesus hype just as all the New Age gurus got on board and started printing their books and escalating the emotions of anyone who would get on the bandwagon, bringing people's expectations to a fever pitch.

Many of Miller's followers gave up their worldly possessions in preparation for this imminent return of Jesus and were left penniless when the prophecy failed to come true. When the projected day came and went, the scramble to reinterpret the date took place and, on more than one occasion, the new projected dates failed to yield the appearance of Jesus. See Millerites on Wikipedia for further explanations and details about the movement.

In 1957, social psychologist Leon Festinger proposed what is known as the *Theory of Cognitive Dissonance*. His theory was based on the study of a group of people known as Seekers who were sold on the idea by a channeler, who was the head of the group, that a certain group of aliens would come and whisk them away in a spaceship on a certain date at a certain time. When that date came and went and no spaceship appeared to take the devotees away to the stars, another date was set, then another date was set after the second date failed to manifest the prophesied alien pickup. Like the Millerite movement of the 1840's, many of these people had liquidated all their worldly possessions in the belief that when the spaceship came to pick them up they would no longer need them. Just like the Millerites before them, these people were left penniless in the aftermath of their own form of great disappointment. The case study of this group of people can be read in the book *When Prophecy Fails: A Social and Psychological Study of a Modern Group That Predicted the Destruction of the World* by Leon Festinger, Henry Riecken, and Stanley Schachter published in 1956.

Festinger's study focused on this group of Seekers and how they individually dealt with the disappointment and the cognitive dissonance that occurred within their psyches when their firm beliefs were shattered. Some people just chalked it up to being gullible and sheepishly moved on with their lives, trying to pick up the pieces and recover their psychological loss. Others, however, went through a series of psychological gymnastics in order to irrationally maintain their belief system despite the fact that none of their beloved prophesies came to be. In a sense, they went into a form of cognitive denial, just as many of the Millerites and other groups did when Jesus failed to appear on the many projected dates of his return throughout our history. Through this form of cognitive denial, the study group fabricated any number of excuses as to why they were never picked up; they were not devoted enough to deserve to be taken away, or the aliens had other business that was more important to attend to at the time, but would return when their other more pressing business was completed, or any number of irrational excuses for why it didn't happen - but still might.

This same type of channeled chicanery has been dished out by the alleged Galactic Federation of Light for almost 30 years and people still keep falling for the alien rescue ploy, and they make excuses for why these bogus prophecies handed down through channelers to these anxious believers never seem to manifest. This is a repeating pattern in the modern New Age arena and, as evidenced by Festinger's case study in 1954, humans have been fooled by these same false prophecies channeled down by alleged aliens for a couple of generations now.

This type of irrational rationalization is the same as that experienced after the disappointment over the many projected returns of Jesus since about 500 CE. Now that the 2012 Mayan prophecy has basically fallen on its ass, we find ourselves once again at the juncture of another Great Disappointment, only this time it affects the New Age spiritual arena more than the Christian bailiwick.

Now that the prophesied Mayan date has come and gone, we find those still hooked into this wishful-thinking belief system scrambling to project new dates for this presumed mystical global shift in consciousness. It seems that the human psyche is addicted to mystical happenings to solve all of our problems, even reaching for pseudo-scientific explanations to provide a basis for this continual mystical illusion and keep it in place. The latest irrational rationalization that came about as a result of the 2012 disappointment was a new projected date of late September 2015 for this mystical shift in consciousness put forth by Dr. Simon Atkins. The proposition of moving the failed prophecy date out further because of lack of manifesting is the same tactic used by Festinger's Seekers to try and keep a false belief system alive despite repeated evidence that it is all just a gigantic hoax. And, as expected, Atkins predictions utterly failed to manifest like all of the other previous prophecies about some kind of Divine or alien salvation.

All one has to do is Google 'shift in consciousness' to discover that the fascination with the mystical rollover in human consciousness is alive and well, despite the cognitive dissonance that resulted from the 2012 disappointment. The psychology of human beings that causes us as a species to continually look outside ourselves for some kind of spiritual salve to fix all our woes is alive and well, and that is what keeps religions and mystical spirituality going as an industry. In both of these arenas, there are two major things lacking. One is a sublime lack of common sense, and the other is a total lack of pragmatism. In order to advance into higher levels of human conscious awareness, one must have both of these qualities in order to not only see the problem, but to arrive at a cogent solution as to how we advance our cognitive awareness beyond such escapist tendencies.

Millions of people worldwide know that there is something inherently wrong with virtually all of the systems that currently govern this planet, and it is not just governments that are at fault. We find that no matter where we turn for answers of spirit that there is nothing presented to us as a solution other than mysticism and religious supernaturalism, yet over the course of our entire history, neither of these arenas have provided any type of answers beyond pie in the sky beliefs and selling mystical hopes and dreams. Neither system has *ever* delivered on its promises.

Having said that, and showing an inherent weakness in human desires for the mystical, many of us are cognizant of the fact that humanity can no longer progress on the path that our history has shown us. We are seriously in need for advancement in our consciousness, what some people call enlightenment. Where we continually fail ourselves is when we buy into belief systems that magical, mystical or supernatural events are going to bring this about. It is readily apparent that our species has developed a handicapping dependency syndrome attached to the mystical or supernatural traditions to provide the solutions we seek to solve all the ills of the world. This syndrome started with the so-called gods and our forced dependency on them to solve all of our problems. From religion it moved into esoteric or occult mysticism, and although mysticism seems to present itself as an alternative to religion, the dependency on forces outside ourselves is still the mainstay of the belief system.

With the modern New Age movement, aliens have been thrown into the mix as one of the elements of our 'salvation' from ourselves. No matter where we turn we are met with external solutions and, unfortunately, most of us have not wised up enough to realize that none of these external solutions has *ever* manifested, nor will they. It is the stark insecurity of present human consciousness that keeps us all believing that we are not personally powerful enough to overcome all the human obstacles that plague our world that keeps us ever searching outside ourselves for a solution. This book is designed to empower your consciousness in order for you to realize that there is no external solution, no mystical or supernatural force that is going to bring about the change that our species consciousness needs to make at this point in our evolution. If there is going to be a shift in consciousness, we are each individually responsible for making that change within ourselves.

If you are reading this book, then it is assumed by this author that you have gone down the dead-end road to mystical solutions and found them all lacking. If you are reading this book, chances are that you know, on some deep gut level, that there is more to the spiritual equation than the spiritual malarkey peddled in the marketplace, but you have also realized that nothing in the purported spiritual arena is remotely feeding that inner hunger to know the truth. Reading the material on the bookshelves is nothing but a continual rehash of the same tired old doctrinal bullshit, with all sorts of gurus telling you to meditate but not telling you why, or what you are ultimately seeking to achieve. They can't provide the answers you seek because they don't have any more of a clue about real spiritual advancement than you presently do. They are ignorant hucksters capitalizing on selling hopes and fear and offering nothing but mystical hogwash as a solution.

Every religion on the planet operates from the foundation of the carrot and stick approach to enforce the beliefs of their respective faiths. You must go the way of their gods or you will wind up in some kind of hell, or be persecuted through some form of karmic lowering of status in your next life if you don't perform the will of the gods as their dedicated servants. You are expected to perform the rituals, pay obeisance, pay tithes, pay the priest, pay for the sacrifice, pay, pay, pay. The question you have to ask yourself is whether you want to continue to pay into bullshit systems of mystical beliefs or whether you are ready to start collecting your birthright as a free and independent consciousness.

I have already written a number of books called *The Evolution of Consciousness* series. All the books in that series are like tutorial manuals to lead one to understand not only what the spirit path is, but also explain how to get there. There are going to be references in this book that can be found in more detailed explanations in those books, but that are also necessary in providing explanations in this book that are designed to pull the true seeker after spiritual understanding back on track after the 2012 disappointment. As with the books in *The Evolution of Consciousness* series, this book is being written outside that series in order to redirect those who still have a keen desire to understand spirit, but who are also fed up with the circus called New Age spirituality and the mystical hype some authors are still trying to sell to make their egos feel valid in an arena that has absolutely no validity as it is currently being sold.

I did not write this book before now, although much of the information contained in these pages has been in my possession for a lot of years, for the simple fact that with all the 2012 mystical hype capturing everyone's imagination, no one would have listened to the message in these pages. It took the 2012 disappointment to take place before most readers would even bother to read a book that remotely countered the mystical 2012 belief system. Now that the mystical 2012 bubble has burst, more people are willing to listen to serious information about advancing themselves, where before, they only wanted to continue to believe in the mystical hype. There are those who are going to continue to chase the mystical rainbow, and this material is not written to try and convince them otherwise, for the simple reason that they are not remotely ready to face reality. There may be some who are wise enough to throw the systems of mystical pursuits in the trash where they belong, but everyone is simply not cognitively ready to deal with the harsh truth. That harsh truth is that you are utterly and completely responsible for yourself and your own cognitive advancement. No gods, no aliens, no mystical cosmic switch is going to be flipped to help you advance your cognitive awareness. It has never happened and it will never happen. To believe such things is only deluding yourself with wishful thinking. To advance your own cognitive abilities, to step into *enlightenment,* takes hard personal work, and relegating the responsibility of doing that work to some mystical solution will only leave you wanting.

2: The Real Story of Siddhartha Guatama

Probably the first recorded instance of an enlightened human being on this planet is the story told about Siddhartha Guatama, or Buddha. The term Buddha itself means awakened one, or enlightened one. To understand the basis of the term as an 'awakened one', the first question we have to ask is awakened from what?

As I explain in depth in my book *Willful Evolution*, humans virtually all operate from a singular form of consciousness. Although our ideas and beliefs may vary from person to person, we all think within a framework of predetermined reality that was passed down to us by our parents, and was passed down to them by their parents, all the way back into the far reaches of time. We live in a predetermined and accepted framework of defined reality, and anything that goes beyond that reality, say a sixth sense for instance, automatically brings us into conflict with our rigidly enforced definition of reality. To reach enlightenment, as it is called, requires our awakening from this limited perception of reality, what I call the first cognition, and advancing our consciousness into a higher level of cognitive awareness, what I call the second cognition. This awakening from the 'sleep' of the first cognition and advancing into the higher level cognitive awareness of the second cognition is what people refer to as enlightenment. There is nothing mystical about this process, and one only achieves it by hard, personally gut-wrenching work.

No one progresses into the second cognition without having their first cognition perception of reality totally challenged on every front. No one moves into the second cognition without confronting all their ideas about their perception of reality, which ultimately brings about situations of cognitive dissonance. As psychologically disruptive as this process is, it is an unfortunate necessity given the fact that we are all so deeply asleep (cognitively unaware) in our current state of perceived reality. In order to step into higher levels of cognitive awareness, to become enlightened, we have to actively engage in unraveling our current perceptions and beliefs in order to see the truth behind the illusions of our perceived reality.

What is told as the story of Buddha has been greatly mythified by those who came behind him and corrupted his teachings. As the mystical story goes, Siddhartha was the son of a chieftan and Siddhartha was a prince who lived in the lap of luxury at that time. The mythology of his background relates that he spurned the life of luxury and pursued the life of spiritual understanding based on his seeing an aged old man and not understanding the suffering of the lower classes and castes in his own kingdom. When confronted with this misery that surrounded him, it allegedly served as a catalyst that began his search for the reason behind all human suffering and he allegedly started his spiritual path for altruistic reasons. He wound up hanging around with the Hindu ascetics at the time and finally realized that Hinduism in its many religious doctrines did not answer his questions. Ultimately, as the mythology goes, Siddhartha sat under a tree for forty days before his enlightenment came to him.

Subsequent Buddhist mythology that developed at the hands of Brahmanic infiltrators to his teachings, eventually turned the Buddha into some sort of divine being and he was elevated from the position of simply being a cognitively aware human being to near godhood. Through this priestly infiltration and covering up the truth, Buddhism became just another religion with deism, mysticism and the supernatural at its core. The original teachings of Buddha were such a threat to the Hindu religion of subservience to their numerous gods that the Brahmins ordered that all Buddhists should be killed.

Here is the real story behind the mythology. Siddhartha was in fact a prince who did live a life of luxury away from the poor in a remote kingdom of the Shakya clan. His father's kingdom was later usurped and annexed by the Kingdom of Kosala. What goes unrecorded is that the Kingdom of Kosala brought Hinduism with it and did what they could to force the religion on Siddhartha's father, which he ultimately refused to accept. His refusal to force the religion of the Kingdom of Kosala on his people is what eventually resulted in Siddhartha's family being dispossessed and turned penniless into the world. It was this extreme state of cognitive dissonance, resulting from living a life of luxury and security to suddenly being cast out with the poorest of the poor, that was the spark that eventually led to Siddhartha's ultimate enlightenment as the Buddha. He went from the lap of luxury to walking penniless scraping for a meal, and that resulted in a very extreme form of cognitive dissonance. His world as he perceived it was utterly shattered. Everything he thought he knew was gone, so he was left with trying to find a solution as to what happened, why there was so much human suffering, and this prompted to him to search for an explanation.

He did run with the ascetics for a time, until he ultimately figured out that their ways and teachings would never offer any answers, so he moved out of their ranks and finally attained his enlightenment. What Buddha discovered was that all human suffering had nothing to do with their positions or circumstances in life. The root of all human suffering was the limited cognition of humanity, i.e. the ego. The root of all suffering amounted to us being enslaved to all the ideas and beliefs of the first cognition world and that, after he crossed that cognitive threshold into the second cognition, all of his own personal angst and pain disappeared along with his ego personality. Buddha discovered the power of higher level consciousness by defeating his own ego, and he found enlightenment.

In this short historical synopsis we find the basis for the idea of enlightenment and what it actually means. There is nothing mystical about this explanation, and the only reason the institutionalized religion that formed after his death teaches the mystical is because those who subverted his teachings had no understanding of what they meant. In order to explain this in cogent terms from a second cognition standpoint, I want to cover the nine virtues of Buddha.

Before covering these in depth, the reader must understand that I am not a Buddhist, nor have I delved into the Buddhist religion as a practitioner over my own years of study. Modern Buddhism, despite its claims to the contrary, is just another institutionalized religion designed to enslave the minds of humans and keep them from advancing themselves, cognitively speaking. I am going to share these nine virtues with the explanations about what they truly mean without all the mystical bullshit the religion wrapped around the teachings.

The first virtue is when one becomes Awakened. Becoming awakened refers to when a person can finally start to see past the perceptual ego illusion. In order to see past the ego illusions we all embrace, we have to individually challenge what we have been told is real. Our physical reality is real. Where the illusion of the ego comes in is through our perception of reality. We believe many things on an ego level because we are told to believe them. We also believe things because everybody else believes these perceptual illusions to be real, so we find our consciousness bound in a system of reinforced ignorance. So long as we continue to serve and embrace these perceptual illusions, we are allowed a lot of latitude for individual beliefs within that system. Once we have the wisdom and courage to challenge our own perceptions, then and only then can we become cognitively awakened.

The second virtue is Perfectly Self-Awakened. Just as the virtue states, this is a matter of self-performance, which means the burden and responsibility to become self-awakened lies with every individual. One can't become self-awakened if they are looking outside themselves for answers. If you look at every religious or mystical tradition on this planet, they all lead to outside intervention for a solution, just as with the 2012 hype and the external shift in consciousness. No such external source of enlightenment exists, so continuing to search for external solutions to what you can only do for yourself will always lead to disappointments. No one and nothing is going to do it for you, you have to do it for yourself, or do without.

The third virtue is Endowed with Higher Knowledge and Ideal Conduct. When one steps into the next level of human cognitive awareness, they no longer need the laws of the ego world to tell them what is right and what is wrong. The second cognition leads one to know not to do the stupid things that egos do and that one no longer needs laws, presumptions of morals or ethics - all harnesses for rampant egos - to be able to comport themselves as civil beings. Higher knowledge in the second cognition leads one to know ideal conduct without having laws to tell you what is right and what is wrong. One does not need the fear of punishment as the enforcer of one's actions, which controls every ego.

The fourth virtue is Well-gone or Well-spoken. This virtue has to do with the fact that a self-aware being should be able to explain the principles of the second cognition and how others can achieve it for themselves. They do not sell deception or misdirection. They do not peddle mysticism or dependency on sources outside oneself to find one's own power.

The fifth virtue is Wise in the Knowledge of the Many Worlds. As one's consciousness advances, they realize that reality goes far beyond current human perception. They realize that there are in fact many other worlds besides our own; that we are not, and never have been alone in this universe. One realizes that there are multitudes of other worlds, or realms, some physical, some non-physical in which many varied forms of consciousness dwell. So long as we stay roped into our limited, rigidly-defined first cognition perceptual reality, we will never discover these other consciousnesses or these other worlds.

The sixth virtue is Unexcelled Trainer of Untrained People. When one can step into and realize the second cognition, they can see the tools needed to guide others into this next level of cognitive awareness. All of the books in *The Evolution of Consciousness* series are designed to help one progress into the second cognition by teaching not only about the problems, but also the solutions to advancing one's cognitive awareness. Where priests and mystics have deluded and misguided human consciousness for thousands of years, second cognition teachers have all done their best to offer the guidance for others to follow in their footsteps. Buddha, the man called Jesus and Friedrich Nietzsche are three of the foremost teachers that have all been misunderstood by first cognition thinkers.

The seventh virtue is Teacher of Gods and Humans. This virtue is only understood when we can understand that all of our ancient gods were as bound by the ego as are we humans. Since they were as lost in the ego as humans, then even the gods could benefit from the second cognition teachings of an enlightened human being. Buddha may be the first recorded example of an enlightened human being, but because he was human and achieved this advancement in his own consciousness through his own efforts, it means that any human can also achieve this enlightenment, this shift in cognitive awareness for themselves. Buddha was not a deity any more than I am. We both share the same level of second cognition advancement, and you can do the same, provided you stop looking outside yourself for mystical or supernatural solutions.

I put little store in the eighth virtue as I see it as subsequent religious overlay, that virtue being The Blessed One. I see no real need to comment on that as I don't see Buddha as religiously blessed any more than I find myself religiously blessed. Siddhartha achieved his enlightenment the same way that I did and you can too - by doing the hard work of assaulting your ego and moving past its perceptual world of self-enforced illusions.

The ninth virtue is "One with taints destroyed, who has lived the holy life, done what had to be done, laid down the burden, reached the true goal, destroyed the fetters of being, and is completely liberated through final knowledge." First off, let's remove the aspect of the 'holy life' from this list of virtues. Once again, that is a later religious overlay and has nothing to do with the road to cognitive advancement. The 'taints destroyed' are all the poisons of the ego that we all carry. In order to get rid of these taints, one 'must do what has to be done', and that is the hard job of personal self-analysis required to destroy the ego perceptions. Once one can get past the ego, they have 'laid down the burdens' that the ego forces us all to carry to bolster its world of perceptual illusion. When one can surpass the first cognition, one does 'reach a final goal' when they attain the second cognition (although I have no doubt there is more cognitive advancement beyond the second cognition). One doesn't necessarily 'destroy the fetters of being', but one does transcend the limitations of ego perceptions and gets free from those fetters of our cognition. Once one transcends out of the first cognition, they are truly 'free and liberated' from the perceptual world of the ego that keeps our consciousness enslaved to a limited form of tainted reality.

Although brief, these explanations should patently illustrate that there is nothing mystical or religious about advancing one's own perceptual awareness into a higher state of consciousness. If you want a shift in your consciousness, you are personally responsible for making it happen for yourself. No one is going to do the work you are required to do for yourself. To expect any external agency to do this work for you is the epitome of spiritual laziness. You can beg, you can hope, you can pray if you like, but nothing is going to move your consciousness forward except you. If you want it, you have to make it happen. The processes on how to confront your own ego are explained in depth in my book *Demystifying the Mystical*. Don't buy this book if you are looking for some kind of escapist salve to solve your shift in consciousness. The book is for the serious-minded spiritual individuals only, and not for the pie in the sky crowd.

3. Recovering from Cognitive Dissonance

Cognitive dissonance occurs when one's world perception is either challenged or shattered. A major bout of cognitive dissonance, similar to those mentioned in chapter 1, leaves a person feeling very vulnerable from a psychological standpoint. Cognitive dissonance is a particular problem associated with the ego self, for it is the ego that continually buys into the illusions that surround us. Beliefs are one of the worst forms of illusion because beliefs sell the ego hope. Prior to the 2012 disappointment, millions of people were filled with either hope or dread depending on their own ego's perception of reality. Those who feared the end of the world breathed a collective sigh of relief when major cataclysms didn't destroy the world as we know it. Those who placed their hopes in the mystical shift in consciousness, in a sense, had their world destroyed because their fervently held hopeful belief in the 2012 promises failed to manifest in the way they imagined.

This failure of the mystical shift in consciousness to occur created a form of cognitive dissonance in those who had hung all their hopes on that event happening. Part of cognitive dissonance happens when we lose a firmly held belief, or when a hoped for 'spiritual' event doesn't occur, and we find ourselves utterly without a place to turn for explanations. As stated in chapter 1, some people create all sorts of explanations in order to keep their belief structures in place, even though events have shown the belief to have existed on a false foundation. Others simply take the bitter pill and fall back into normal life, because there is no explanation offered by any of their authority figures to explain why it didn't happen.

The failure of the 2012 Mayan prophecy should prove to mankind once and for all that as a species we have to quit hanging our hats on ancient predictions and prophecies. The entire premise for prophecies was established by the ancient gods to keep us ever looking forward to events that were most likely never going to occur. By engaging our attention on such non-existent prophetic happenings, we have completely forsaken our own responsibility to advance ourselves in the present. We have made phenomenal technological advancements in the last 250 years, but our consciousness has not kept up with our advancing technologies, and we are now at a point where, if our consciousness doesn't advance beyond petty ego paranoia and greed, we may wind up destroying ourselves.

The reader must become aware of the fact that all the tales about the ancient gods from the heavens interacting with humans on Earth have a basis in reality. I realize this is a large pill to swallow, but until one can acknowledge this as a fact, we can never understand where we got religions, mysticism and continual prophecies. When we can acknowledge offworld intervention in our past, then we can start to unravel why we believe many of the things we do today, particularly where world religions are concerned. The ancient gods created the dependency syndrome through which humans to this day look to outside sources for all solutions to our problems. This issue of offworld intervention are discussed in depth in my books *We Are Not Alone, Parts1, 2 & 3.*

Under the influence of the ego personality, we are all insecure in an unknown universe. We do not know whether we are alone in the universe or not, and if we aren't, our limited imagination presents offworlders as either predators or saviors. Through either scenario, we presume ourselves to be lesser beings, either threatened or in need of salvation. Much of this mindset can be tracked back directly to religions and the constant battle between good and evil, god and the devil, gods and the demons, etc.

The ancient gods who ultimately wound up in control of this planet about 5,000 years ago created this dependency syndrome for our consciousness. They were not advanced intelligences, meaning that when Buddha attained his second cognition awareness, that even those gods couldn't touch him for the simple reason that they were ego-driven first cognition beings themselves. The only way they were able to rule the consciousness of mankind was through sheer brute force which has turned into multigenerational indoctrination at our own hands. Unarmed with any weapons with which to compete with them, our species had no option other than to knuckle under their tyrannical control. Our planet today is merely a reflection of the psychosis of these presumed gods handed down to the human race through religious indoctrination. Even science itself is nothing more than a reaction to the restraints of religion, so its very basis is founded on religion, or protesting against religion.

Our entire system of perception in the first cognition is nothing but a mirror reflection of the psychologically impaired and insecure gods themselves. There is no overarching consciousness that rules the universe. There is no cosmic Oneness. That is just another handicapping mindset for our consciousness. It is just another escapist mentality that removes the responsibility for individually advancing our own conscious awareness. You have to ask yourself whether you are tired of chasing fanciful mystical notions about salvation and step into full responsibility of facing reality or not. Regardless of how weird some of the ideas I am presenting may be, they will eventually lead the true spiritual seeker to the ultimate ugly truth about our reality, why it is the ways it is, how it got this way, and how we become masters of our own cognitive destiny as a species. If you find you don't have the stomach for that, then put this book down, you do not have the courage or strength necessary to walk this path.

It seems no matter where you look, whether through books or through shows like *Ancient Aliens,* we are constantly being sold the idea about how the gods from the heavens were wiser than us and more advanced than we lowly humans are. You find the starry-eyed proponents of alien speculation elevating these offworld races onto some form of mystical technological pedestal, always expressing the idea that we need them to come back and teach us what they know now that the egos of the proponents think we are ready to understand all their hidden technological knowledge. We human beings have a bad case of species arrogance, and that arrogance is enhanced by academics with their degrees and awards who feel they are able to be spokespersons for everyone on the planet were these aliens to return to our planet. This is the height of ego arrogance.

The fact is that the offworlders who developed the human species on this planet, and their subsequent usurpers were the stuff of nightmares. The last thing we want is to see their return. All you have to do is look at the legacy of human consciousness they left us to figure them out. They demanded subservience, sacrifice and worship to fulfill their own petty ego desires. Our world is but a reflection of their own cognitively impaired psyches. Look at all the religious hatred and wars through our recorded history and you will understand the mindset with which these alien races infected human consciousness. The only escape from that system of limited consciousness is to advance beyond it, where their systems of control can no longer control your own consciousness.

Humanity has followed the mandates of the gods throughout or history. Our entire system of cognitive awareness, from religion to science, is only a reflection of their minds. To understand the mind of god, just look at your neighbors, the gangs, the jihadists, the crusaders, the warmongers and the politicians, for these are the reflections of the consciousness of the gods. Their consciousness is nothing to which we should remotely wish to aspire. As a species we can do better than that. That is why Buddha's virtue about one who can teach the gods is so relevant. Even the gods failed to understand the second cognition, which is why they ordered their Brahmin priesthood to kill all Buddhists. The second cognition is a direct threat to their systems of cognitive control, both on this planet and across the universe.

Through metaphor, *The Matrix* films alluded to this mental prison erected for our consciousness by the gods. Just as the machines within the world of *The Matrix* controlled a sleeping and unaware humanity, the gods maintained control in our reality in virtually the same way. Their agents for control were initially the priesthoods they created. Priests had the power of life and death over any heretic or straying worshipper. This same mindset of destroying the heretics is alive and well in academia, as well as in virtually every government worldwide that seeks to kill the voice of dissent and truth whenever it is voiced. Our entire planet is as much a trap for our consciousness as the machine world of *The Matrix*. It is hidden, yet it is right in front of our face no matter where we turn. It is a prison without fences and boundaries, but it is a prison all the same. The only way out of this prison is to advance your consciousness into the second cognition.

One of the major ways the gods enslaved our consciousness was because they learned how to 'capture' our imagination. They created bogus prophecies that humans either feared or dreaded, and they feasted on the disappointment when these things failed to come to pass. They fed on fear, anxiety and devotion. We keep feeding their system to this day by fiercely embracing our perceptual illusions and being willing to kill rather than let go of the illusions. To advance into the second cognition we have to shed all of these illusions. The greatest illusion of those seeking true understanding of spirit is where we continually externalize and give up our power to fanciful ideas and beliefs in some force outside ourselves that will supernaturally makes us better people.

The 2012 failure turned many people away from the spirit path. It was just one illusion too many, and millions got disenchanted with the spirit process altogether. The great disappointment that resulted from the 2012 failure caused many people who came here to do a job to step off the path entirely. In that respect, the gods won. Millions of people incarnated as human beings on this planet to stop this system of tyranny. These people come from all walks of life and cover many different professions. Each of them came in with a mission to undo this system of cognitive control within their own trades and occupations. Most of them are completely unaware, from the standpoint of conscious awareness, that they have such a mission, but each of them is working within the system to destroy the system by creating something new and better to replace it. This can't be done if we give up on ourselves because one bogus prophecy or another fails to come true. Prophecies *always* fail to come true. It's time we mature as a species and recognize this one profound fact once and for all and move beyond reliance on such prophetic pipe dreams.

If you are reading this book, there is every chance that you came here to be part of this mission to advance humanity. You are not here to save the world like some sort of savior. You can't free any consciousness except your own. If you can't free your own consciousness, how do you expect to be able to show or tell others that it can be done? You start changing the world by changing yourself. If you can't make yourself better, then how can you expect someone else to do it for you, whether it is a god, an alien, or the giant cosmic marshmallow in the sky? You can't take responsibility for anyone on the planet except yourself where your own cognitive advancement is concerned. If you can't accept responsibility for yourself, then why should you expect some god or anyone else to do it for you? If you want to be in charge of your life, you have to take charge, plain and simple. Quit wallowing around in fantasy land and do the work required to advance yourself, or step aside and let the others who will pass you by.

4. The Mission

Many readers may be familiar with the books written by Barbara Marciniak, *Bringers of the Dawn* and *Earth: Pleiadian Keys to the Living Library*. In these books many found a spiritual wake-up call by the so-called Family of Light. Some of the information in those books was highly relevant and honest, but it was mixed with a lot of the New Age doctrine that also served to confuse many of the so-called 'renegades' of the Family of Light. I am going to separate what I found to be true versus what I found to be New Age doctrinal fiction in those books. Many of us are renegades for consciousness advancement. We came in with a plan to alter not just humans on this planet, but the face of this whole universe. Yes, I know, tall order and it sounds quite woo-woo.

The Pleiadians used the simple allegory of the dark T-shirts and the white T-shirts being the bad guys and the good guys in their story. What the Pleiadians that piped down that information to Marciniak failed to mention is that they had their own agenda aside from what we came here to do. Her books are unfortunately filled with the doctrine of docility that pervades the New Age arena; all that hype about the Prime Creator and love and light, blah, blah. I ask the reader to move beyond the doctrine of docility and recognize the fact that we are involved in a war. It is not a war of violence, but a war of conscious advancement in the face of a system that has human consciousness totally locked down in a system of control called the first cognition.

Every renegade is here to fight this war for human consciousness, but we have to individually transcend the tyranny that enslaves our own minds through our own ego perceptions and controls first. If we can't overcome the ego problem within ourselves, we will never succeed in the overall shift in consciousness required to alter the face of the universe. We all came in with the information necessary to perform this individual freeing of our own consciousness, provided we can overcome our ego fears and societal constraints to rise to the mission we came here to do. As explained in *Demystifying the Mystical,* the ego program is a fierce adversary for anyone, and overcoming the programming, and it is a program, takes supreme effort and dedication.

The one thing Marciniak's books didn't explain was the nature of this war. There was too much admixture of New Age doctrines contained in the books to get a clear view of the mission objective. This book is designed, in part, to clarify what that mission is and what it requires of you to make it work. The Marciniak books were written with multiple layers of understanding that can only be found as one advances their own cognitive awareness. Most readers did not get past the first level of information and bought into the whole light warrior paradigm without an ounce of understanding of what it truly meant. Buying into the idea that they were special and giving lip service to the idea of being a light warrior appealed to egos. It gave the ego something to latch onto to make it feel special, and the ego is all about feeling special and different, i.e. superior. I can guarantee you that the vast majority of readers never progressed beyond this superficial understanding of the doctrinal information contained in those books. Their petty egos filled their heads with illusionary images of being light warriors and they were off to the races proclaiming how special they were, cloistering together and patting themselves on the back about being light warriors with that doctrine of docility wrapped around them like a warm blanket.

The ego program is like quicksand. Just about the time you feel you are starting to exit the program, it sucks you right back in. Marciniak's books are filled with multi-level triggers. If you are one of those people who happened to read those books, and if you felt energized after reading certain passages in those books, that heightened feeling of energy was a result of the embedded triggers in the material opening up access channels for information within you. Unfortunately, for most people, the quicksand of the ego sucked them right back in and they bought into that sense of feeling special by calling themselves light warriors and they never moved beyond that point in their development. Any subsequent reading of the book, provided anyone bothered, would have prevented the next level of embedded triggers from activating, for each level of triggers required a level of conscious advancement to benefit from them. If one remained stuck totally in the ego program, access to these subsequent layers of triggers was prohibited.

The Pleiadians were totally up front when they told the readers that they were going to trick them and deceive them. Few readers understood this statement and, unfortunately, took everything in the books at face value. They bought into all the hogwash about the goddess and love and light. Many egos started claiming that they were Pleiadians and only wanted to go home, etc., etc. This is pure ego escapism and self-glorification. If you came here to be part of this mission for advancing human consciousness and you got yourself roped into that New Age belief system because it made your ego feel special, you need to pull your head out of your ass and get with the program. You are failing in your own personal mission objective.

This is a war, and to succeed you have to adopt a warrior's mentality. This means that you have to realize that this planet is a battlefield and the enemy - the entire ego system of the first cognition - will destroy you if you let it. You will be nothing more than a cognitive casualty to your own ego and you will be utterly ineffective as a warrior with a mission. When you let your ego kick your ass, the enemy has already defeated you and you are no longer a warrior, you are part of the problem.

I am not here to mince words and play nice with your ego and its petty belief systems. Given the nature of this war for human consciousness, why do you feel that you should be mollycoddled because it makes your ego protest? Your ego is your greatest enemy, and I am not going to talk nice to the adversary in your head just because it gets its feelings hurt. If you are in fact a warrior here on a mission, then you by god need to buck up and get with the program. *There are no reinforcements.* You are here, you are on the ground, so stand up and do what you came here to do. This mission will continue with or without you. Only you can decide where you stand in this equation. You are either in our you are out. You volunteered to come here and do this. Honor your obligation, quit whining and stand up to the challenges that face you in this endeavor. If you can't personally do this, then all your ego bravado about being a light warrior is nothing but hollow braggadocio, and you deserve no notice whatsoever other than as a laughing stock. You are a paper tiger, with a mouthful of bravado and not an ounce of internal fortitude to do what you came here to do.

So, what's it going to be? Are you going to continue to play games of escapist fantasy, needlessly hoping that some mystical force is going to come save you from yourself because you are simply too lazy to do it yourself, or are you going to rise to the real challenge you came here to accomplish? The love and light agenda has solved nothing. It is nothing but feel good tripe to soothe egos that need to feel wanted, special and part of a herd. To be a true spirit warrior, you can't follow the herd. You have to be strong and independent. You have to have the guts to face all adversity, especially the adversity of overcoming the ego program within yourself. If you don't have that kind of internal drive or strength, then stand down and go live a meaningless life in the world of the cognitively dead, firmly rooted in the first cognition. You are free to remain a slave to that system, but in making that choice, don't expect me or others like me who are here doing what they came to do to humor you and massage your ego and tell you that everything is alright. As I said, in playing that game, you are part of the problem, not part of the solution.

5. Turning the System Around

In order to attack and change the system, the system itself has to be identified. If you have been on the spirit path for any length of time, you have finally realized that no matter where you turn there are scores of questions and very few valid answers. It doesn't matter if you turn to the religious, spiritual or mystical solutions, or whether you seek to find answers with the academics and scientists, you have discovered that you are surrounded by brick walls where human consciousness is concerned. We find rigid belief structures controlled by defenders of the particular faiths that are embraced by human egos. There is absolutely no flexibility in this rigid system of thinking and beliefs.

The more educated the individual is, the more rigid their own egos become to protect their perceptual illusions. The fault does not lie strictly within the precincts of religious believers. Everywhere you turn you encounter nothing but defensive posturing and denial used as the weapon to safeguard the territories of the ego. The Pleiadians in the Marciniak books called us 'system busters'. The first cognition is the system we are here to crack wide open.

As I explained in *Willful Evolution,* when it comes to the present system of human cognition, we find absolutely no alternative to that cognitive system of control other than a turn to the mystical. I have already explained that what Buddha tried to teach humanity was a form of true cognitive freedom presented in the second cognition. His teachings, as well as those of Jesus and Friedrich Nietzsche were totally misunderstood by the rest of humanity because they were not explained as simply as what I do in my books.

The Yaqui shaman, Don Juan Matús of Carlos Castenada fame was a cognitively advanced human being as well. We are unfortunate indeed that passing on his teachings was left to a superstitious, ambitious and egotistical fraud artist, for had there been honesty and true understanding about the teachings, much of the New Age mysticism would have been circumvented. I don't recommend reading Castenada's books for the very simple reason that they are rife with supernatural fictional tales that never happened, thereby cheapening very profound teachings about the second cognition. Also, most people who read these books concentrate on the drug use advocated in the books as well as the mystical fantasies concocted around don Juan's teachings. I honestly feel that very few people have developed a keen enough sense of discernment to tell the real teachings from the bullshit stories Castenada fabricated in order to turn himself into one of the first modern New Age gurus.

The system of the first cognition, the system of the enemy, is tyranny, and that tyranny is perpetrated by every ego on the planet in one form or another. Every ego is a tyrant. Every ego's world revolves around itself and its own selfish desires. As I explained in *Willful Evolution,* every culture, every society, every religion and every institution, including governments and academia, are all nothing but expanded versions of the tyranny of the individual ego. Everywhere we turn we find a tyrant. So long as you are controlled by your own ego, you are just another tyrant. To see the face of the enemy, look in the mirror.

The New Age crowd with their doctrine of docility believes that they can love their adversaries into the light, but the fact is, they will still be trying to love their enemies into the light when the tyrants of this world stomp their deluded docile heads into the ground. We are not going to win this war for the advancement of human consciousness through practices of moral ambivalence or mystical feel-good avoidance of the problems that confront us as warriors. The entire doctrine of love and light is being intentionally sown by certain forces on this planet who want a docile population they can put under their subjugation. I personally don't care if you choose or refuse to believe this. It doesn't alter the truth one way or the other. By buying into these mystical doctrines you are only making yourself an unwitting casualty to people who will have no problem cutting your throat before it's all said and done.

Many of the New Agers do not want to admit the level of tyranny that surrounds every human on this planet, or if they do admit it, they are foolish enough to think that their love and light doctrine will somehow insulate them from the tyranny as the global systems collapse. This mindset leaves them totally unprepared to deal with the adversity of a global financial collapse, which is a very real and present danger. Their mindset is no different than Christians who think Jesus will magically appear and whisk them away to heaven at the last minute so they don't have to face the gross unpleasantness of such a scenario. Both of these mentalities are nothing more than ego escapism. Neither of them are real, but that doesn't keep people from deluding themselves with these dreamlike belief systems.

If you feel that you are one of those who came here to participate in this mission to advance human consciousness, you are going to have to develop a very high level of common sense and pragmatism. You are not going to be able to continually play the game of rainbows and butterflies if you remotely intend to achieve your own personal mission goals. There is not an ounce of spiritual pragmatism in believing in fanciful notions or mystical concepts of external salvation. You are going to have to get tough and develop a mental steel that you have yet to imagine exists within yourself, for it is only through advanced cognitive awareness that you are going to be remotely prepared for what lies ahead.

It is easy to deny that this planet is in shambles. It is easy to deny conspiracy theories, and it is apparently easier to buy into bullshit belief systems that make your ego feel good. It is easy to remain part of the herd, to not color outside the lines, to remain a touchy-feely light hugger, but to be a true spirit warrior, all of this must go by the wayside. There is no room for bullshit on the battlefield, so if you came here to do a job, you better get your head in the game because this is not going to be a walk in the park.

Had I written this book before 2012 there would scarcely have been a person who would have listened to the harsh words I am delivering. As it is, there are still too many wrapped up in the smarmy, gooey New Age belief system that all they will be able to do is cast aspersions because I am not playing nice and soothing their stupid egos. If you are truly a spirit warrior, it's time to man-up and quit dancing around in the daisies with all your New Age submissive pals. Those of us who came here to do this job are in every profession on the planet, from the low to the high. Every one of us came in with specific mission parameters. Some are whistleblowers, some are teachers, some are healers, some are investigators and reporters of the truth hidden behind mainstream lies. Because the level of tyranny on this planet is so pervasive, we have to assault every fortress of first cognition defenses. We have to challenge the academic institutions, the religious institutions, government institutions, and we will eventually have to confront the tyranny of the ego in our friends and families as this war for human consciousness progresses. But before any of us can do that effectively, we have to destroy the tyrant in our own minds.

We do not challenge the system through advocating violence. We challenge the system by sowing awareness and knowledge. We challenge the system through our own altered actions by becoming alternate examples of higher level consciousness and how we operate differently than all the current systems of tyrannical mind control that surrounds us at every turn. When we defeat the ego we grow into a state of being fearless, and that fearlessness will show itself to those still immersed in a world of fear. We are here to lead by example, not by doctrinalizing, becoming ego-driven demagogues, or forcing others into just another dead-end belief system. We are not in a position to tell others what to do, for that decision ultimately resides within every individual, but you have the power to change it within yourself, and it is up to you to make that change.

If you feel that you are a spirit warrior, or feel that you have the makings of one, then it is high time you get off your ass and put your money where your mouth is. Quit giving lip service to the idea and start changing yourself to be an example and guide to others. Stop thinking what you believe and start believing in yourself. If you can't do that, then you are not what your ego makes you think you are. You are simply an ego clown going through the motions, living a charade.

The subtle wake up calls have been issued and most are still lost in the maze of the ego. This is not a subtle wake up call. This is an in your face wake up call. Either get off your ass and do what you came here to do, and be a big enough person to admit that all your New Age pulpit pounding is just ego bluster. You have to *choose* to try and make a difference, or be nothing but a sad joke to the serious spirit warriors. Either stand up or sit down. There is no middle ground in this war. You are either in our you're out. Only you can decide which it will be.

Nothing else really needs to be said in this short book. If you want to see a shift in consciousness on this planet, you are going to have to be that agent for change. There are no reinforcements coming from on high to do the job you volunteered to do. You will either heed the call or you won't.

When the final tally comes about, you are only accountable to yourself and you have to live with your decision.

The Evolution of Consciousness Series

Book 1

A Philosophy for the Average Man: An Uncommon Solution to a World Without Common Sense by Endall Beall

Book 2

Willful Evolution: The Path to Advanced Cognitive Awareness and a Personal Shift in Consciousness by Endall Beall

Book 3

Demystifying the Mystical: Exposing Myths of the Mystical and the Supernatural by Providing Solutions to the Spirit Path and Human Evolution by Endall Beall

Book 4

Navigating into the Second Cognition: The Map for Your Journey into Higher Conscious Awareness by Endall Beall

Book 5

The Energy Experience: Energy work for the Second Cognition by Mrs. Endall Beall

Book 6

We Are Not Alone – Part 1: Advancing Cognitive Awareness in an Interactive Universe by Endall Beall

Book 7

We Are Not Alone – Part 2: Advancing Cognitive Awareness through Historical Revelations by Endall Beall

Book 8

Advanced Teachings for the Second Cognition by Mrs. Endall Beall

Book 9

We Are Not Alone - Part 3: The Luciferian Agenda of the Mother Goddess by Endall Beall

Companion Volumes to The Evolution of Consciousness series

Operator's Manual for the True Spirit Warrior by Endall Beall

False Prophecies, Reassessing Buddha and the Call to the Second Cognition by Endall Beall *(Previously published under the title* Recovering Spirit After the 2012 Disappointment: Spiritual Pragmatism Beyond the Realm of Mystical Fantasies*)*

Spiritual Pragmatism by Endall Beall

Revamping Psychology: A Critique of Transpersonal Psychology Viewed From the Second Cognition by Endall Beall & Mrs. Endall Beall

Second Cognition series

Book 1

The New Paradigm Transcripts: Teachings for a New Tomorrow by Endall Beall & Doug Michael

Book 2

Breaking the Chains of the First Cognition: Tools for Understanding the Path to the Second Cognition by Endall Beall & Doug Michael, with additional text by Mrs. Endall Beall

Future Volumes in this series

The Energetic War Against Humanity: The 6,000 Year War Against Human Cognitive Advancement by Endall Beall

Calling All Healers: Healing for the Second Cognition by Mrs. Endall Beall.

Made in the USA
Middletown, DE
13 July 2016